All Scripture references taken from the KJV of the Bible unless otherwise indicated.

SOULS in Captivity, Dr. Marlene Miles

Freshwater Press, USA

freshwaterpress9@gmail.com

ISBN: 9781960150-17-2

Paperback Version

Copyright 2023 by Dr. Marlene Miles

All rights reserved. No part of this book may be reproduced, distributed, or transmitted by any means or in any means including photocopying, recording or other electronic or mechanical methods without prior written permission of the publisher except in the case of brief publications or critical reviews.

SOULS in Captivity

Freshwater Press

USA

Beloved I pray above all things

that you would prosper and be in health
even as your soul prospers.

3 John 2

Table of Contents

The *spirit* of Captivity 6

Who is Responsible? 9

The Devil Steals Souls 14

The Devil Sells Souls 20

Buyers of Souls 21

The Captive Soul 24

Are You A Captive? 30

Freedom 36

Signs That Your Soul Is Captive 41

How Will You Live? 47

Symptoms Of Captivity 51

Bad News 54

Failing Temptations 58

But I'm Saved 60

Rejected Kings 62

Trespassing 64

Blind Witchcraft 66

Forgiveness 69

Prosper It All 73

Emotions 76

Unprospered Souls	78
A Well-Ordered Soul	82
The Dead Yard	84
Command Our Souls	86
PRAYER OF RELEASE	92
Warfare Prayer	96
Healing Prayer	103
Dear Reader	107
Christian books by this author	108

The *spirit* of Captivity

David said, *"In sin did my mother conceive me."* And he said was born into iniquity, (Psalm 51). We are born into the Earth where Satan is the prince of this world; sin is on the menu all day, every day and again all night. It's a 24-hour diner full of sin.

Of course, some people don't believe in anything spiritual. Some believe in some spiritual things, but too many don't believe that anything spiritual could happen to them, except only good things. Even while they are believing all that, spiritual things are happening to them right now, all day every day and all night.

The greatest trick of the devil was convincing people that he doesn't exist. Therefore, it is impossible for anyone who believes in the impossibility of the devil to believe that a man's soul could be *captured* by a non-existent entity who *says* that he doesn't exist.

A captured soul can lead to a controlled body and a captured spirit. And this is a spiritual disaster.

Everyone wants freedom and liberation. Throughout history people have longed and screamed, marched and died for freedom from slavery, bondage, captivity and oppression.

Externally--, from others.

But they have not considered that *spiritual* freedom is necessary, obtainable and … may need to be the **first step** they take toward external, natural liberation.

Many times, it seems that they believe they already have spiritual freedom--, even in the cesspool of their sin.

What a deception.

If man is so well able to deceive *himself*, no wonder the devil is able to capture souls, torment souls and also block the prosperity of souls that should be prospering in the things of God.

Who is Responsible?

Who is responsible for your **soul prospering**? It depends on how you look at soul prosperity. Some define it as the things that God has given your soul, peace, joy, happiness contentment. That's good, but the Bible mentions a few things that leads me to understand that we, ourselves are responsible for prospering our own souls. I believe that we will be evaluated on how we are doing in that endeavor, both now and in the future, even in Eternity. The visit of God to see how you are doing in prospering your soul is evidenced in *that* and how God blesses you. Not the evidence of blessings, but that God blessed you and not another entity *gave* you things.

Is the fragrance you are wearing from God? Or is it the knock-off from the devil? If it is not evident immediately, it will be told in the long run.

If you allow the Spirit of God to conform you to His image and likeness, then your soul will prosper. I see that as man, being made new every day based on what we will accept into our lives, day by day—what we choose.

And what we will reject, what we will not accept changes who we are. We should be growing day by day from glory to glory, strength to strength and from faith to faith and from prosperity to prosperity--, of all kinds.

> I call heaven and earth to record this day against you, that I have set before you, life and death, blessing and cursing: therefore choose life, that both thou and thy seed may live:
>
> Deuteronomy 30:19

I'd never argue with God about gifts, the gifts are His and He *gives* them to us, so there is nothing to complain about. Gifts of the Spirit, Fruit of the Spirit –or anything He wants to give to any of us--, no complaints. But those are things we need. They are things we need in order to prosper our souls, and **we** should be prospering our own souls.

The Word says in Luke 21:19, in your patience, *possess* ye your souls. We are given a mandate to possess our souls. That means don't let anyone or anything else POSSESS it. We are to ***possess*** our own souls, confirming that souls are possess-able. We are in charge of what happens to our souls.

Note here that Patience is a Fruit of the Spirit; we need the Gifts of God to fulfill His mandates to us.

In your patience ***possess*** ye your souls.
Luke 21:19

That every one of you should know how to possess his vessel in sanctification and honour; 1 Thessalonians 4:4

Now may the God of peace Himself, Jehovah Shalom, Yahweh Shalom, sanctify you completely; and may your whole spirit, soul, and body be preserved blameless at the coming of our Lord Jesus Christ.

Blameless.

May God himself, the God of peace, sanctify you through and through. May your whole spirit, soul and body be kept blameless at the coming of our Lord.
1 Thessalonians 5:23 NIV

So, we have responsibility regarding our souls. We are spirits who live in a body, and we have a soul. We have a soul that needs to be protected, possessed by us, matured and prospered. There would be no reason that God would give us a soul if we were to just ignore it. We maintain our bodies, physically and we feed our spirit and soul with the Word of God, in prayer and in praise and worship. Our souls also need ministering to.

The Devil Steals Souls

People foolishly trade their souls in devil deals all the time. Why? Ignorance—sometimes they are duped. Rebellion. Disobedience. Impatience. Greed. Pride. Desperation. Any of the aforementioned, and other reasons, such as:

- Ignorance: Perhaps they place no value on their souls.
- Greed, or pride: They want something so badly that their unprospered soul with its natural mind and carnal desires wants something so badly that they are

willing to trade *anything* for it, their left arm, their first born, their right leg--- their very souls for this *something*. They are impatient; they can't wait until God gives it to them the **right way.**
- Desperation: They believe they are at the end of their *hope* and there is no other way to get the thing(s) that they want or *feel* they must have.
- Sometimes a seemingly innocent transaction can be a soul-stealer. Pray the Lord will reveal devil tricks and traps to you, so you are not deceived. Some include eating food or beverage that may defile a person. Once a person is defiled, their soul is easier to capture.
- Sometimes items of yours can be taken (stolen) and placed on evil altars. This may result in your

spirit/soul being summoned against your knowledge, or even against your will, while your body sleeps. Evil exchanges can be made this way. Of note, when a soul is captured, that is the most evil of exchanges: the person that God intended to have a good life is on spiritual lockdown while the enemy is living that person's life. Granted, messing it up royally, but living that human's life.

Keep up with your personal items they can be misused to indoctrinate you against your knowledge, even against your will, into evil.

Stay out of sin, the fleeting pleasure of sin can bring **years**, even *decades*, or a lifetime of negative repercussions. For example, **you should only have sex with your spouse that you are legally married to.** Period. Anything else is inviting all kinds of hell. It may not be noticeable at first, but over the years it will become apparent. Sex (fornication, adultery, and other perversions) is a very common path of exchange, devil deals, open doors to soul snatch, and I don't mean any of this in a good way. Yeah I'm saying to keep up with even your bodily fluids. God did not give us sex as a plaything.

Plan B is not the issue. You need PLAN G (God) from the jump, else Plan D, the devil could whip up on your for most of, if not all of your life.

For the lips of a strange woman drop *as* an honeycomb, and her mouth *is* smoother than oil:

But her end is bitter as wormwood, sharp as a twoedged sword.

Her feet go down to death; her steps take hold on hell.

Remove thy way far from her, and come not nigh the door of her house:

Lest thou give thine honour unto others, and thy years unto the cruel:
Proverbs 5:4-5 and 8-9

For what shall it profit a man, if he shall gain the whole world, and lose his own soul? Mark 8:36

When God breathed into the nostrils of man, man became a living soul. Your soul, like the breath of life that sustains you is on loan from God. When your breath is gone, it's lights out. When the soul is gone, what makes you, *you*—what makes your personality is gone. If you are still vertical, you are essentially a robot. God designed you to serve and worship Him in your own unique way, not as a robot.

Other reasons people may barter with or sell their souls:

- They don't plan to live Eternally. Perhaps they don't think they will need their souls after this life, in Eternity. But they will.
- Some have lost their souls because they were SOLD OUT at birth, at conception, or even before then. That is possible because we really don't know what our ancestors have done. Ancestral sin and evil foundation are booby traps awaiting too many unsuspecting souls that are born onto this planet.
- **Most people sin their way out of their souls**. Either because of the sin down their family line or they, themselves have sinned. ALL of us have sinned and fallen short of the glory of GOD, so none of us can judge.

The Devil Sells Souls

The devil sells souls. He acquires them probably by hook or crook and then he sells them.

The souls of men should not be up for sale, but here's the passage from the Bible:

> And cinnamon, and odours, and ointments and frankincense, and wine, and oil, and fine flour, and wheat, and beasts, and sheep, and horses, and chariots, and slaves, and souls of men.
>
> Revelations 18:13

Buyers of Souls

Why would anyone want another person's soul? Why would anyone want your soul?

A person buys a soul so that soul becomes a slave, a captive, a prisoner to the person who bought the soul.

A soul has great value and power. It is from God, surely the devil would like to rip God off.

There are a lot of things in the Earth that a disembodied spirit cannot do, without a body. By capturing a soul, an evil spirit has captured your body. Now the evil entity can do evil in the

Earth again. I say, again because that evil spirit has lived for ages and for many lifetimes. It has possessed or influenced or oppressed many souls. This spirit entity probably thinks it is having fun, eating, drinking, drugs, sex. Under its influence, maybe you think you're having fun, too. You've never been this popular before. But what starts out as fun, won't stay that way. It will turn into evil and to destruction sooner or later.

God has given Earth to man. Any spirit needs a human to operate in the Earth realm and he operates as a man or through man.

You can be manipulated when your soul is controlled; you are on REMOTE, so if your soul is under the devil's command, the devil gets a BODY to do illegal things in the Earth. The only way the devil can do things in the Earth is illegally or take over a body or influence (bribe) or trick evil human agents.

So under devil control, you're like a ROBOT because you have a body, the very thing he needs, and he's taken it over, now your authority to act in the Earth realm is given over to the person that is controlling your soul. The devil has acquired a person's soul and also their body and also their God-given authority. There is a lot of power lost by the human in that transaction or takeover.

There is so much you can't do with no soul, or with a damaged, fragmented, crippled soul. You cannot fulfill your purpose, your destiny, your whole reason for being here spiritually crippled.

The Captive Soul

By keeping your soul captive, locked away, separate from your being –, your spirit and your body, the soul, the thing God gave you to make you alive, the devil is trying to take it from you. Can this be a clue as to what the devil wants to do to mankind?

Your soul, the part of you that communicates via your spirit man with God's Spirit is separated from the man and this is part of how the detention is maintained. This is especially possible if you don't even *know* that you are captive, or that some **part** of you is captive. Depending on where this part of your soul is being detained, the Word of God may not be able to reach it. The Light of Jesus Christ doesn't reach it. The washing by the water of the Word, doesn't reach it. It is sequestered away under guards, (tormentors). As long as you don't know that you're captive it is as though you are going along with the program. As long as a person goes along with the devil's program for whatever reason, either thinking there is a payoff for them, or out of fear, the devil will be successful in this kidnapping of the soul.

For example, your heart could be captured by the enemy in any number of ways. Unforgiveness. Bitterness. Resentment. Jealousy. Simple: when you don't forgive, a part of your heart is now no longer available to love, or to participate in life as usual. Bitterness, the same thing, only worse. You still love this person and that person, but *that one* you just can't stand. A part of your heart is blocked off, closed, locked down. It is fragmented and unusable by you.

Resentment and jealousy, every time you see that person that stole your spouse anger rises up in you and you feel horrible. That part of your soul, your heart, is captive and just seeing the person whom *you allowed* to cause it torments you. A part of your heart, your soul is captive and being tormented. Of course, the devil will make sure you see or think about this person often so the torment can continue.

Soul ties cause fragmenting of the soul as well, it's why God doesn't like them. A soul-tied soul is also captive for many of the reasons as above, resentment, hurt, bitterness, jealousy. *What's he doing now? Who is she with now?*

Why?

> For I perceive that thou art in the gall of bitterness, and in the bond of iniquity.
>
> Acts 8:23

Of course, the devil is mean, but this torment opens the door for **more** evil to come into your life and it opens the door for **more** of your soul to be fragmented, stolen away, and locked away.

Sounds fantastical? Nope. The more you hurt, the more you don't want to hurt. The more you will be ashamed, afraid, hide and possibly swear off relationships ever again. This keeps *divine connections* away from you. This keeps blessings away from you, this keeps you separate, lonely, and probably unsuccessful. This could keep destiny helpers away from you and it could keep you away from people that you are supposed to be a destiny helper to.

This goes on for a while, maybe too long--, possibly years, now you've *blown* purpose. The devil got another one. Time to move on to another soul, another life to ruin. If it wasn't you whose life the devil derailed or destroyed, please don't let the next one be you.

When it's all said and done here on Earth, what will you to tell the Angel at the Pearly Gate? What will you say to God at the White Throne Judgment when your works will be tried by fire? Your works will be tried.

Do you have works? Will you have works?

What will you say to God as you are presenting your soul, providing you have it back and all intact by then?

Are You A Captive?

When a soul is *owned by* or in debt to the devil, he owns your whole life... He makes a suggestion; you think you thought of it. Like an infomercial in the Garden of Eden the devil silently whispers or loudly yells into your ear – depending on your relationship with him. I say that because if you don't have a relationship with God, then you are practicing your relationship with the world, and the *god* of this world is Satan. It is by default that Satan is your *god* if you have not willfully chosen the Lord Jesus Christ as your Lord and Savior.

Those who say they are agnostics or atheists are deceived; choosing no one is the same as choosing the default *god* of this world, Satan. *That* you don't believe in something does not make it so and your disbelief doesn't stop it from happening to you. It only means that you will be in more disbelief, akin to astonishment when/if it happens to you.

If you haven't chosen Jesus and also renewed your mind, then you are listening to, entertaining and doing devil suggestions because that is what comes to you 24/7. Yup. Even while you are asleep. Maybe *especially* while you are asleep.

Unless your peers are saved and sanctified, peer pressure can be devil pressure.

Let's go race our cars on the Interstate.

Let's go to the graveyard tonight and sleep there.

Let's go to a tarot card reader….

Whatever the world suggests, whatever the world is selling is an *option* to the unsaved, unprospered soul. And he doesn't see anything at all wrong with it. If you had any idea how many people are going on "vacation" to see diviners or order up witchcraft you wouldn't step foot on another airplane unless you are completely prayed up.

As long as you are captive, the devil is running your life until you can get free again--, *if* you can get free again. Some don't and they die in captivity and go to hell. Isn't the purpose of captivity to sell that soul or terminate it? The devil is not playing, people.

A person could die, finally knowing or never knowing that their whole life was spent in spiritual ***captivity***.

So many people don't know they are captive. But they can still do ungodly things in the Earth realm, like have 14 kids with 8 baby mommas and never think that there is anything wrong with it. That's got to be because of demonic remote control because who logically—, in their right mind would do that?

A sinner doesn't know that they are sinning until the Law is preached to them.

The devil doesn't bother some who are captive because they might find out that they are captive and then seek GOD and start praying for real, in earnest. What if you really start seeking God, who is able to save to the uttermost. God, who can deliver them and set them free. **Hallelujah!**

Whom the Son sets free is free indeed.

GOD can set you free. GOD can deliver you from **anything** if you want & ask to be delivered. If you are serious about it. It may take some work; it may take some time. It will take repentance, renunciation, dedication, devotion, prayer, fasting, resistance, attention to the disciplines of God. And just reading that list it may make you wonder why would you ever want to step away from God if it takes that much to get back to Him?

Surely you know that the devil will put up every obstacle and roadblock he can to keep you from God. He will try to block you from reaching God. He tries to block the Word of Truth from getting to you. And once captive, surely he will try to keep you from ever getting free, from ever getting BACK to God.

It is so much easier to STAY with GOD than it is to walk away and then fight the devil and his minions to get back to God. But it can be done, don't lose heart. God welcomes you back with open arms. Every time.

Freedom

Just the list of all it may take should make the average person not ever want to step away from God EVER.

NO ONE WANTS TO BE CAPTIVE; everyone wants to be free. Especially since war criminals take prisoners for trade or to terminate them --- it's not for play-play.

- Even people who THINK they are powerful and have made deals with the devil are actually CAPTIVE whether they know it or believe it or not.

I can imagine how a person's heart must sink when they find out the devil was lying to them all along. Maybe they got something out of the devil-deal – maybe the didn't. Maybe they thought they were at the height of power – they weren't; they are captive.

There has got to be a time in their life (or death) that they realized not only were they deceived, but HOW deceived they were for power, works of the flesh, money, or revenge--, all the things a childish, immature, *unprospered* soul would want in life, or out of life. Even though they may have been doing evil things to other people they were still just pawns of the devil. It's the evil that the devil wanted to do, that's why the devil agreed to it. **It wasn't for you; it was for him.**

- Those who are having fun, living it up, got everything they think they want in this life – if GOD is not the Head of their life, they are also CAPTIVE.

And he spake a parable unto them, saying, The ground of a certain rich man brought forth plentifully:

¹⁷ And he thought within himself, saying, What shall I do, because I have no room where to bestow my fruits?

¹⁸ And he said, This will I do: I will pull down my barns, and build greater; and there will I bestow all my fruits and my goods.

¹⁹ And I will say to my soul, Soul, thou hast much goods laid up for many years; take thine ease, eat, drink, and be merry.

²⁰ But God said unto him, Thou fool, this night thy soul shall be required of thee: then whose shall those things be, which thou hast provided?

²¹ So is he that layeth up treasure for himself and is not rich toward God.

Luke 12:16-21

As I said before, if you don't have Godly protection, if you are not walking toward God, with God, toward God, in Christ, then you don't have any real protection against anything that the devil comes up with.

We are put here to serve God, to worship God. Whomever is not serving God is serving another master. It can't be Sunday, God and the rest of the week, do as your friends do, or whatever you want. The excuse that work is so cut-throat, that you have to behave another way Monday through Friday is **not** serving God. It makes you a hypocrite on Sunday and a carnal, worldly person the rest of the week.

It's one or the other, not both. Or the other master has control of him, and he cannot /does not seek God. ... he is captive, in his soul.

If we look at the Body of Christ, we see it is full of sickness, division, fear, poverty and lack. There are serious character flaws in people who *say* they are Christians. This is all indicative of *unprospered souls* and **souls in captivity.**

Souls are not prospering in captivity; they can't. This is one of the main reasons why Jesus came to Earth to take our captivity captive. Jesus did what He was supposed to do. Jesus did what He came to Earth to do but have we received it? Are we walking in it?

> Turn again our captivity, O LORD, As the streams in the south. They that sow in tears Shall reap in joy. He that goeth forth and weepeth, bearing precious seed, Shall doubtless come again with rejoicing, bringing his sheaves with him.
>
> Psalm 126:1-6

Signs That Your Soul Is Captive

When a soul is captured spiritually, there is usually zero natural evidence of the captivity unless a discerning person knows what to look for. Sometimes the person cannot see himself as captured because *he **is** captured*. This is where one-another ministry comes in. This is where the five-fold ministry gifts come in. Someone will tell you if things aren't quite right with you.

Foremost, the sign that a person is captured is frustration, delays, restrictions. He can't seem to get ahead, try as he may. He may not be trying anymore, however, he may have already given up. This is what the devil wants.

I insert here that too many men are running, running, running away from great women and avoiding marriage because they don't want to be "trapped", not realizing that the reason they have locked marriage and God's will out of their plans and out of their lives is because a part of their heart **is already captured** by evil; it is not available for real love. No woman will ever be able to "trap" them because the devil already has these men "trapped", captive. They will not fulfill God's will for their lives in marriage and having righteous seed (children).

Here are some signs that your soul is captive in case you're wondering if you are.

The Devil loves Trauma: a major trauma or disappointment, loss, broken heart—anything that has traumatized you significantly even to distraction is a door open. It opens the door for the devil to fragment or capture your soul. And then he will do it again and again to take more and more of your soul, especially if you don't heal from it the first time.

A major trauma can hinder a person for a long time, ESPECIALLY IF WE STAY THERE in that trauma. And *especially-especially* if WE REHEARSE IT either over and again in our minds or verbally to anyone who will listen.

Once a *spirit of captivity* has taken root in your life, YOUR LIFE CAN CHANGE dramatically, drastically.

They can end up with a *Victim Mentality*, they expect the worst. They can seclude themselves and become lonely, adopting a what's the use attitude.

Apathy may follow, then they may go into a DEPRESSION, and that is a way the devil can get **more** of your soul.

Yes, there is Salvation--, thank You, Jesus and there is Deliverance –, it is the children's bread. But you still have to PROSPER your soul. We can't just leave it the same as it was when we came into the Earth as kids or into the Kingdom as new creations.

Be renewed by the renewing of your mind. Let this Mind be in you that was also in Christ Jesus.

A *spirit of captivity* will destroy purpose, it will destroy destiny, it is not in line with godliness. Because of deliverance, demons may be gone, but they have left a permanent imprint on you. Perhaps they left a stain or a mark on you because you were once captive. And now you behave differently than you did before you were ever captive. But you don't realize it. We all need to be completely set free by the LORD. Amen.

> I beseech you therefore, brethren, by the mercies of God, that you present your bodies a living sacrifice, holy, acceptable to God, which is your reasonable service. And do not be conformed to this world, but be transformed by the renewing of your mind, that you may prove what is that good and acceptable and perfect will of God.
> Romans 12:1-2 NKJV

Apostle Paul pleads with us to keep our flesh under submission to the Spirit of GOD. Don't sin. With all that is in you, don't sin, as much as it is in us, by the help of the Holy Spirit, don't sin. And let our minds be transformed- as we are made *more* into the likeness and image of Christ. Look we already had a head start at that- we were created in the image an LIKENESS of God. God said, Let US go done and make man in our own image and in our likeness, – but then man fell.

He fell into sin.

But then Jesus came, and He picked us back up; thank You, Lord.

How Will You Live?

Let God transform us into a renewed mind, into a new person by changing the way you think. Think on these things, things that are lovely, pure and true and have good report. These things will help your soul to prosper.

If your identity and your sense of who you are in God is captive, you cannot reach destiny.

Are you asking *Where is God?* God didn't go anywhere. Perhaps you're captive. Why can't you sense God anymore, or as you used to? What's happened to *y'alls* relationship? Could you be captive?

Your **Worship, prayer life, and Bible reading have also dwindled to nothing or almost nothing.** These are signs that you may be captive.

This is what the devil wants. Dry you up and keep you away from God. But you have to <u>stay connected</u> to God; He is your lifeline. The Spirit of the LORD connects to your spirit and your spirit man ministers to your soul, and then your soul to your body. If you are not connected to GOD – how shall you then LIVE?

If you start asking questions such as, *"What am I doing here?* Then you know you're captive.

If your prayer life, has dried up, esp. spiritual warfare is dried up... you are probably captive or some part of you is. You're a person who has never done spiritual warfare? You are probably captive, or some part of you is. **A person who won't even START SPIRITUAL WARFARE** if they are captive. They've got a lousy excuse day by day as to why they can't do spiritual warfare. They are probably already captive.

There is no reason God would give us the whole armor of God in the Book of Ephesians if we weren't supposed to be doing spiritual warfare. There is no reason for Jesus to be the Captain of the Host of the Armies of the Lord to take us into battle and give us victory unless we are supposed to do warfare. Spiritually speaking.

If you feel as if you're in A DESERT, DRY – NO WORD FROM THE LORD. EMPTY you are probably captive because we don't live by bread alone, we need the proceeding words of the mouth of God. We need to hear the LORD and we need to hear Him to LIVE.

You've got no word? You're most likely already captive.

Hiding? Lost, feel lost, or Confused? Lost your courage and spiritual vision and purpose seems like it's gone? You are probably captive.

Seriously, this is a good time to do a spiritual checkup – let's get this year going the right way!

You need prayer? Do you need to fast? Do you need deliverance?

Symptoms Of Captivity

- Sickness
- Disease
- Poverty

You're captive because all of the above is under the Curse of the Law.

- Fear
- Frustration
- Loneliness
- Nothing is working out for you. you get almost there and then you get pulled back.
- Tormenting Evil dreams
- Can't sleep/TORMENT
- Gnashing of teeth.

- Monitoring spirits- you are sensing their presence.
- Worse, you are being fed in the dream. You are captive.
- Being defiled in the dream, no that is not free relations, that is defilement. You are captive. When a person is captive the captor can do anything, they want to them, at any time.
- Sleep paralysis or worse, you are captive.
- Inconsistency in your life, you can't seem to get ahead
- Seeing STRANGE PEOPLE in your dreams
- SPIRIT SPOUSE(s)—those are not treats or perks; you are captive.

In your waking life, you feel as though you are a robot and that you are just going through the motions. You do things that are so out of character for you. You do dangerous, ridiculous, terrible things and then later wonder why you did those things. You may be captive

People who "black out" come to mind, they just woke up and they were I a place doing a thing and they don't know how they got there. They don't remember even having done it. And yes, I'm going to say it, an ID discovery type moment and don't know how they got there or what they did. That is FULL POSSESSION. That's full captivity.

Bad News

    I will take this moment to say that the news is bad, and it bothers me. The news we see online and on tv, etc. What kind of news do you think that is when EVERYTHING is horrible, horrible and terrible?

    What is being reported is the antics, tactics, activities and demonics of demons—working through people. Working through the bodies and souls of people who are *captive*.

You see it, read it You can't believe it. You SHAKE YOUR HEAD because how can there be this much bad news and in so many places?

My question is since there is DNA *WHY* are people still committing crimes? It seems so 1800's to me.

OH, because of demons – the demons don't have any DNA. What do they care if a sinful, captive, rebellious against God, disobedient soul goes to real prison, or worse?

They can just go get another one since the devil sells souls!!!

Can anybody out there hear what I'm saying?

Since we are going into spiritual warfare, demons have to be named, pointed out, accused of what they do, spiritually speaking. But in a natural world, they report all of this bad new when they are just celebrating demons. A rotten person won't care if they get good attention or bad, as long as they get attention. A person bent on fame won't care if they get good press or bad press, as long as they get press then they feel relevant. All this bad news is the reporting on demons while blaming it on *people.* Blaming it on unprospered souls who unwisely go about the Earth, they go about their so-called lives with no godly spiritual protection and some of them get caught up in the most evil, the absolute most evil.

Demons don't get accused of anything, the perpetrator of the crime or horrible deed his life is now in shambles or completely over because his unprospered soul that the perpetrator was toting around in his body was a prime target and of great value to the devil. The devil captured that soul and used it to the max, for evil.

The greatest fear of all these horrors is that evil is being normalized.

Failing Temptations

An unprospered soul is weak and easily acquired by the devil. An unprospered soul fails pretty much *every* TEMPTATION test and gets SNAPPED UP, ENSNARED and TRAPPED by the devil.

Walking about in the Earth with NO godly spiritual protection is the most unwise thing a person can do.

If the soul of an unprospered soul is weak, it probably is also very weak in will power as well. Intellectually, it may be lacking, not knowing spiritual things, even if he or she is a book genius.

My people are destroyed for a lack of knowledge. Hosea 4:6

But I'm Saved

The devil is doing what he wants with captive souls. You may be one who believes that nothing like this can happen to you. You're saved? OK, then what is happening? Why is this happening? Why are all of these things in the Bible about this sort of thing, if it *can't* happen?

Why is the Psalmist repeating over and again to be released from prison? Delivered from the tormentors? Uncaged? Released from jail, the pit, and from slavery? A lot of the Psalms were written by David Can we say that

David didn't know the Lord. Really? Of course, not!

But why is this happening?

And how is this happening if I'm saved? Yes, a person can still sin after salvation. It is not recommended, but it can still happen. We all have sinned and fallen short of the Glory of God.

But his is happening for any number of reasons. SIN is the main one. Sin by you or someone in your ancestral line opened the doors to allow spiritual captivity. Or the *spirit of captivity* is in your family line. Sin, disobedience and rebellion against God.

Please note: Rebellion is as the sin of witchcraft.

What warfare do you think Jesus was talking about all through the New Testament?

Rejected Kings

> For rebellion is as the sin of witchcraft, and stubbornness is as iniquity and idolatry. Because thou hast rejected the word of the LORD, he hath also rejected thee from being king. 1 Samuel 15:23

    Let me take a minute to exegete the lasts part of that passage regarding rebellion and witchcraft. Even though this message was written to Saul, Jesus is the **King of kings,** and we are *little k kings* in the Earth. But when we rebel, when we are disobedient or rebellious against God, when we fall into witchcraft or idolatry, then we are also rejected out of our *little k kingship*, by the Lord. That is a horrible place to be because we lose our authority, and it looks like it gets taken over by the enemy.

Worse, having lost authority makes us helpless. It makes us helpless captives in the hands of an evil entity who hates us and wishes us no good.

Trespassing

However, in some captivities or attempts at captivity, spiritual kidnapping of a soul-, sometimes the devil is mistaken and wrong, we have to call it out, go into spiritual warfare, open our mouths, call it out, declare and decree and rescue that soul from the hell of devil torment.

When the soul is repentant and crying out to God, we can go into warfare for their sake and get that soul out of hell. Sometimes that someone is ourselves when we come back to our godly senses. Praise God.

Sometimes the devil does have legal right, but we take him to spiritual court by doing spiritual warfare, plead our case to our Most Merciful Father and get released from captivity, torment and hell while our bodies are still living here on the Earth.

We have to do this in our authority, in the authority of Christ. This is no time to lose power, influence or authority in our Christian walk.

Could be the enemy is totally trespassing, but he may not be. Either way, you just need to open your mouth, pray, declare, decree.

Blind Witchcraft

The Spirit of the LORD God is upon me...Isaiah 61:1

Every person who has suffered an emotional blow, a trauma, or has experienced the pain of **a broken heart is almost certainly being held captive in some area of life.**

Anyone who comes from a broken home, or from a history or a family line of the occult or blood shedding at the hands of a family member, or someone in your bloodline is **most likely also captive.**

Without forgiveness, sometimes we do these lockdowns ourselves. We lock ourselves down with that spirit of captivity. When we say we're **NEVER GOING TO FORGIVE SO AND SO,** we are locking ourselves down in to captivity. When we say WE ARE NEVER GOING TO FORGET THE THING THAT HAPPENED we are putting ourselves in captivity *and* turning the lock on the door ourselves. Don't do that!

WORSE, WHEN WE PRACTICE WITCHCRAFT AND START WISHING EVIL ON THE PERSON WHO DID US WRONG OR WE *THINK* THEY DID US WRONG.... ESPECIALLY WHEN WE PUT A **NEVER** OR AN **ALWAYS** or an **every** or an every *time* on EVIL WISHES – and we declare them out into the future, THEY BECOME as DEMONIC

INCANTATIONS, making you a blind witch.

>STOP IT!

>Repent.

Forgiveness

Forgiveness is messy – look at all that Jesus went through for us. Jesus had the power to forgive sins on Earth. And, He has given us the power to forgive. It takes a power; it is not easy. It is messy.

Don't start none, won't be none— BUT maybe you didn't even start it.

Look at all Jesus went through on that Cross for us. I say all this because today I want to talk on SOUL PROSPERITY, but the Spirit of God took this book the way He wanted to go. The reason for it is we <u>need</u> to hear what the Spirit has to say. We need soul prosperity, but as long as we are captive, our soul – which is comprised of our EMOTIONS, our WILL and our INTELLECT is on lockdown, we've got a problem. So first, we have to be *set free* first to prosper.

No one can prosper if they are in captivity. No one can prosper in times of war. Joseph, you might say. No, Joseph was already prospered in his soul. The beauty of Joseph and Daniel was that they maintained their soul's prosperity even in captivity. That in itself is another great feat that takes the Grace of God, because without God that is impossible.

Beside the rivers of Babylon, we sat and wept
as we thought of Jerusalem.
We put away our harps,

hanging them on the branches of poplar
trees.
For our captors demanded a song from us.
Our tormentors insisted on a joyful hymn:
"Sing us one of those songs of Jerusalem!"
But how can we sing the songs of the
LORD
while in a pagan land?
Psalm 137:1--4

If war is declared against you by the devil – there will be no soul prosperity during that time of war. But isn't that the goal? To keep your soul from prospering in the things of God?

If you have declared war on someone that you should have forgiven, but you've decided to never forgive them, your soul will not prosper the whole time that you are in unforgiveness. Bitterness is a progression of unforgiveness and that is neither a time of soul prosperity either.

A soul cannot prosper in survival mode (except by God).

A soul cannot prosper in a war situation, (except by God).

Prosper It All

To prosper in one's soul all three aspects of the souls should be prospering.

1. Our emotions – is mostly what I'll talk about today.
2. Our will – we should endeavor to have a Godly will. To want what God wants. To do what God wills us to do. We can find that out in the Bible, it's written there. Start with the Ten commandments in the OT and Jesus said A NEW

COMMANDMENT I give you – so the commandments are not over.

You get an amendment or an addendum to your credit card contract whenever the bank wants to send it, don't you. OK, so the commandments were not over at the time that Jesus said that. Further, GOD is still talking, so...

3. Intellect. If we have the Mind of Christ, we can think like GOD. God's ways are not our ways. His thoughts are not our thoughts. As we access the Mind of Christ, then our INTELLECT will be prospered. God says that He would not have us ignorant so let's prosper our intellect.

Hosea 4:6, My people are destroyed for a lack of knowledge. So we must dent our ignorance and prosper our intellect.

In all your getting, get understanding. Solomon wrote all those Books of Wisdom and asked God for Wisdom, and we need that too, right *little k king*? (Read one chapter of Proverbs a day.)

Emotions

THE EMOTIONS make a huge impact on our SOUL's PROSPERITY. Yeah, I'm saying, **GROW UP**. Christ grew in stature and favor with God and men. He GREW, why can't we?

Immaturity and childishness is one of the main signs of an unprospered soul. We should no longer be thinking and acting like children now that we are taller. Now that we are older. It is not becoming, it is not befitting, it is not Godly because there is no love in it.

When I was a child, I talked like a child, I thought like a child, I reasoned like a child. When I became a man, I put the ways of childhood behind me. 1 Corinthians 13:11

We are to keep our flesh under and CAUSE our souls to grow up because left to our own devices, most people will take the easiest road, sometimes that's the wide road of destruction that everyone else is taking.

Unprospered Souls

Let's look at some unprospered souls in the Bible to get a baseline. Basically any evil king: SAUL, who wanted to kill David. HEROD, who wanted to kill Jesus as a baby.

Nabal was a wealthy man, but he wasn't a kind or godly man. For the first time I can see how money can't buy you love in the sense that the love of God was not in this man's heart even though he was wealthy. His behavior was that of an unprospered soul, so who are we to say how he received his wealth or from whom?

> A certain man in Maon, who had property there at Carmel, was very wealthy. He had a thousand goats and three thousand sheep, which he was shearing in Carmel. His name was Nabal …surly and mean in his dealings—
>
> 1 Samuel 25:2

Naaman was a commander in the army of the King of Aram, who was not a good king. Naaman went to Israel to be healed of leprosy by God, through Elisha. He was healed. Elisha did not take money from Naaman, but Gehazi, Elisha's servant ran after Naaman to get an offering from the commander, even though he was told not to. Disobedience is a sign of an unprospered soul. Greed and lying are both signs of unprospered souls. Unprospered souls are easy pickings for the devil.

Gehazi ended up with Naaman's leprosy, into his generations. Disease is a Curse of the Law; disease is a sign of a captive soul. See how the Gehazi failed the temptation of money and goods.

Joseph's 10 older ½ brothers were evil and unprospered in their souls. They wanted what they wanted when they wanted it. That's a sign of an unprospered soul.

JOSEPH was prospered in his soul; he was very prudent.

JOB was prospered in his soul; job's wife – not so much.

JESUS was prospered in His soul.

Why do you want to be prospered in your soul? Because the Word says so. To make right and godly decisions, choices. To stay out of trouble. To help others who may be in trouble.

To be pleasing to GOD. To avoid temptations. To stay out of the clutches of the Devil by falling into temptations.

To keep from being captured or captive by the devil or by evil

An unprospered soul is easy pickings for the devil, but it is STILL a soul. It still have a great value but if the devil gets his hands on it and he can program it for evil and pure evil that's the worst thing that can happen.

A Well-Ordered Soul

Knowing how to keep it all together and not be fragmented by devil traumas, traps and tricks takes Wisdom and the Grace of God.

If that does happen, being able to gather up all the parts of yourself and move forward, not lingering in the past, not leaving parts of your in the past—in old relationships, at former friends' houses, at ex-s houses, in the street because of hatefulness and all those works of the flesh that causes souls to fragment. It takes power. It takes the Grace of God ad Grace is a Power.

If you fall into the devil's traps and become fragmented, by the time you get to where God wants you to be, IN LIFE you are a whole person. You can fulfill destiny, ministry, purpose. You can live a good life and e a good family person, minister properly to your spouse and children and leave a good legacy in the Earth.

You are not a piece of a person or a shell of a person, a part of a person, frustrated, miserable, ineffective, that's what an unprospered, captive person is.

The Dead Yard

Then there are some who get saved and never plan to change their souls. They don't plan to change anything because they don't think there is anything wrong with them. The only get saved so you have a place in the dead yard after death out back, behind the church, maybe.

They think they can keep on living life as usual thinking they've got an insurance policy for burial; I mean a place to put the body. Further, they've convinced themselves that they WILL get in those Pearly Gates. We are supposed to present our souls, blameless --, when we get to those Gates how do we know that is not the admission to get in? Will the state of our souls be considered in order to get into the Pearly Gates?

Beloved, I pray…

Command Our Souls

We can command our souls; we can talk to our souls like the man in Luke with the barns full of fruit and harvest. Or we can leave our souls on the couch for days and day and wonder why it's not getting better or why our life is not getting better, or why it may be getting worse.

We can require things of our soul, change, growth, prosperity. Say, *"Soul, you can do better than that!"*

Or we can require nothing of our souls if we don't believe that evil things can happen to Christians. Let me say that *Christian* was not Jesus' last name, Christ was not Jesus' last name it was His anointing. And what do you think you need an anointing FOR? It is to take action, do work. You need anointing to do ANYTHING in the Earth, successfully. And the Christ anointing is the most powerful anointing that there is.

So, tell your soul to prosper, demand that it does better and become more like Christ every day; that is how a soul prospers or else, it will remain Unprospered.

GOD said to prosper it, possess it, maintain it, and present it. And, if we think about it, as a Garden. 1 Thessalonians 5:23 -- GOD said to present it…. The garden of your soul, like Eden for Adam, like Eden for Eve – your soul you are assigned to tend it, dress it, be fruitful, multiply it's virtues, it's beauty, it's goodness, it's authority and purpose in the Earth.

JESUS: did. Jesus Fasted. Prayed. GREW in the favor with GOD and Man. Worked. Healed. Helped. Fed. Blessed. Forgave. Forgave. He Forgave some more. He Slept. Rebuked; ministered to all who asked. That is how Jesus *"dressed"* His Garden that God put Him in.

God came down in the cool of the day to see how Adam & Eve were doing with their souls – BAAAAD. They got kicked out of the Garden.

But God said of Jesus, ***"This is My Son in whom I am well pleased."*** Don't you want God to say that about you?

How are you doing with your soul?

You brag on your job, your car, your house, your husband, your kids…

HOW are you doing with your soul up to this point? Let's make our boast in the Lord, but how is it going with your soul these days?

God's ways are not our ways, His thoughts are not our thoughts, they are much higher. But, why all this talk of being brought out from affliction in the Word of God?

> Isaiah 61:1 The Spirit of the Lord God is upon me, Because the Lord has anointed me
>
> To bring good news to the afflicted;
>
> He has sent me to bind up the brokenhearted,
>
> To proclaim liberty to captives
>
> And freedom to prisoners.

Why all this talk in the Bible about captivity and prisons and prisoners unless there is something to it?

To open blind eyes,

To bring out prisoners from the dungeon

And those who dwell in darkness from the prison. Isaiah 42:7

To hear the groaning of the prisoner,

To set free those who were doomed to death,

Psalm 102:20

It shall come about on that day,' declares the Lord of hosts, 'that I will break his yoke from off their neck and will tear off their bonds; and strangers will no longer make them their slaves.

Jeremiah 30:8

Bring my soul out of prison,

So that I may give thanks to Your name;

The righteous will surround me,

For You will deal bountifully with me.

Psalm 142:7

Both the spirit and the soul can be fragmented. How are you doing? Are you doing as well as you think, HOLDING IT ALL TOGETHER through life's hurts, pains, losses, sudden traumas, sudden destruction, broken hearts? How are you doing? Are you holding on to all of them? Have you decided in your heart that you will never forgive? That's not good.

Have you decided in your heart that you will never forget? Also not good.

If the Lord has delivered, ask Him to renew your mind so you do not dwell in the past and your soul can prosper.

> Remember ye not the former things,
> Neither consider the things of old.
> Isaiah 43:18

WHOM THE SON SETS FREE IS FREE INDEED John 8:36

PRAYER OF RELEASE

Father, I repent for every sin I have sinned against you, for all rebellion, disobedience on behalf of myself and my bloodline in the Name of Jesus.

Father, forgive me for every sin I have committed against You, knowingly in rebellion and unknowingly in ignorance in the Name of Jesus.

Every power of darkness that has gathered against this prayer, I command confusion to you now and I command you to scatter and do not reassemble, in the name of Jesus Christ.

Any delays against my prayers be struck down now in the Name of Jesus.

Holy Spirit of God, show me if there are any areas of my soul in captivity. Show me where those areas are, I the Name of Jesus.

Father God please show me all sins which enabled parts of my soul to be handed over to the devil for torment, in the Name of Jesus.

Lord, for any and all regions of captivity where there is any part of my humanity, I ask you to send the Anel of the Lord to encamps around us and deliver me, deliver my soul from prison, deliver me from captivity. Lord, return my captivity in the Name of Jesus.

The Angel of the LORD encamps all around those who fear Him, and delivers them"

Psalm 34:7 NKJV

I now speak to those parts of myself in captivity and declare:

Come forth in Jesus' name.

Come forth in Jesus' name.

Come forth in Jesus' name.

Thy word is a lamp unto my feet, and a light unto my path.

Psalm 119:105

Bring me out of darkness, Lord back into your marvelous light.

Lord Jesus, give me Scriptures to light the way so I can come out of captivity.

(Pray whatever the Lord puts on your heart here and even in your Heavenly language.)

Warfare Prayer

Father, Lord, I thank You for the power to tread on serpents and scorpions, and over all the **power** of the enemy, in the Name of Jesus. Your Word says that whatsoever we bind on Earth shall be bound in Heaven and whatsoever we *loose* on Earth shall be loosed in Heaven.

In the whole armor of God, and the Blood of Jesus

Every force of darkness assigned against me life from my birth, even before my birth, catch fire now in the mighty name of Jesus Christ.

All personal material of mine representing me in any or every coven of witches, I command you to catch fire now and burn to ashes.

Councils and counsel of the kingdom of darkness to frustrate my prayers, I frustrate your councils and your counsel in the Name of Jesus.

Lord, as I move from Strength to strength give me victory in these prayers in the Name of Jesus.

Every evil load, evil yoke, yokes of backwardness, immaturity, arrested development hindering my progress, spiritual, soul and physical progress, be broken by the Thunder hammer of God now in the Name of Jesus.

Father every captivity that is disallowing my purpose, ministry, destiny or dreams to be hindered or block, return that captivity now by the power in the Name of Jesus.

I call my destiny out now in the mighty name of Jesus.

Every prison door, gate, lock, that is built to block, stop or hinder me from making a successful life, career and marriage I command it to fall now after the order of the wall of Jericho in the mighty Name of Jesus Christ.

Powers limiting my greatness, expire by fire now, in the mighty name of Jesus Christ. I decree that I will not allow evil of any kid against me in the Name of Jesus.

I reject all evil of every kind in any disguise, masquerade or by any power. Blood of Jesus answer any power that is too great for me in the Name of Jesus.

Powers attempting any other member of my family in bondage received the judgment of fire, now in the mighty name of Jesus Christ.

Ancestral bondage that has helped my family. Captive for years. We break free from you now. And the name of Jesus Christ. I command you to release us now. In the name of Jesus Christ.

I break the curse of cursed feet. Over my life, my career. Our family in the name of Jesus.

Powers of hell. Holding me, my spouse or my children? And any. demonic prison cage. Pet. Or lock down. I command you to catch fire. Command the locks to be opened now. And the doors flung open. The name of Jesus.

satanic personality that is found that he shall not release me from Evil prisons or captivity, I command you to die. To perish after the order of Pharaoh, in the mighty name of Jesus Christ.

Captivity I've found myself in, as a result of the location I'm living in, I set myself and my family free. In the mighty name of Jesus Christ.

Every evil captivity I found myself in as a result of fake friends and unfriendly friends--, I set myself free. And I set my family free. All in the mighty Name of Jesus Christ.

Captivity that I found myself in as a result of where I was born or how I was born.--, because of my last name. I set myself free and my family free, in the Name of Jesus Christ.

Captivity of my spouse, my family, my children. That has been tied down to any altar of darkness, I demand that you catch Fire and burn to ashes, now, in the Name of Jesus.

Powers that have vowed that nobody will excel in my family or bloodline,. I decree that you are a liar. And we shall have good success, in the Name of Jesus, by the Blood of Jesus, Amen.

Lord, build a wall of fire, a mountain fire around me. And I declare, no weapon formed against me shall prosper, in the mighty Name of Jesus Christ.

Every one of my blessings that has been held captive by Satanic altars, I command them to be released now, in the Mighty Name of Jesus Christ.

Anything of mine that has been locked up in satanic strong rooms, I decree: Lift up your heads or you gates. Lift up your heads for the King of Glory to come in. Open and blessings come out and come to me, in the Name of Jesus.

Satanic spells used to hold destinies, trying to keep me bound from fulfilling destiny and my family. I command you to lose hold of our lives in the mighty Name of Jesus.

Wizards, warlocks, and evil priests, I command you to scatter, in the Name of Jesus. And never reassemble against me or my family again, in the Name of Jesus.

Darkness, where the destinies of people are destroyed, I command every unrepentant evil priest to be destroyed by the consuming fire of the Lord, in the mighty Name of Jesus Christ.

Every blessing that belongs to me, my family, or the people over which I have stewardship, that's been held captive, I command those blessings to be released now, in the Name of Jesus.

I demand from the enemy restoration of every blessing stolen from me now, 7-fold, in the mighty Name of Jesus Christ.

Healing Prayer

Lord Jesus, release the captive souls. Restore them, heal them and send them back where they belong. Lord, let the rightful owners of those souls begin to prosper and lead the life that You intended for them, in the Name of Jesus.

Lord, please minister to my wounded soul; wash me, cleanse me with living water. Nourish me with the bread of life.

Please restore and put back into alignment all pieces that were held in captivity. Pour in the healing balm of Gilead, the balm of the Comforter --the Holy Spirit and cause your healing to radiate all around through spirit, soul and body.

> The LORD is my shepherd, I shall not want. He makes me to lie down in green pastures; He leads me beside the still waters. He restores my soul; He leads me in the paths of righteousness for His name's sake.
>
> Psalm 23:2-3, NKJV

The LORD is my shepherd. I will not listen to the voice of a stranger again. I will not follow the voice of a stranger. The LORD restores my soul.

Lord, destroy all prisons of captivity, in Jesus' Name, Amen.

> Bring my soul out of prison, So that I may give thanks to Your name; The righteous

will surround me, For You will deal bountifully with me. Psalm 142:7

I seal these prayers decrees and declarations in every realm, age, timeline and dimension, past present and future to infinity in the matchless Name of Jesus Christ.

AMEN.

Related video messages: Dr Miles YouTube Channel

The Devil Loves Trauma, *The Motherboard- message on Soul Prosperity,* **Soul Captivity** (based on this book)

How the Devil Steals from You,

Related Books (all by this author, on amazon/Kindle)

The Motherboard, Souls in Captivity, Soul Prosperity: Your Health & Your Wealth

Dear Reader

Thank you for acquiring and reading this book. The devil is sneaky and subtle so let this book make a difference in your life so you are wise to the enemy's tactics.

By all means prosper and be in health as your soul becomes more glorious and Christ-like day by day.

In Jesus' Name.

Amen.

Dr. Marlene Miles

Christian books by this author

AK: The Adventures of the Agape Kid
AMONG SOME THIEVES

Ancestral Powers

Barrenness, *Prayers Against*

Battlefield of Marriage, *The*

Beauty Curses, *Warfare Prayers Against*

Behave

Blindsided: *Has the Old Man Bewitched You?* https://a.co/d/5O2fLLR

Churchzilla, The Wanna-Be, Supposed-to-be Bride of Christ

Collective Captivity, *Break Free From*

Courts of Marriage: Prayers for Marriage in the Courts of Heaven (prayerbook)

Courtroom Warfare @ Midnight (prayerbook)

Curses of Blind Men

Demonic Cobwebs (prayerbook)

Demonic Time Bombs

Demons Hate Questions

Devil Loves Trauma, *The*

Devil Weapons: Unforgiveness, Bitterness,...

The Devourers: *Thieves of Darkness* (Book 4)

Do Not Swear by the Moon

Don't Refuse Me, Lord (4 book series)

Dream Defilement

The Emptiers: *Thieves of Darkness* (Book 1)

Every Evil Bird

Evil Touch

Failed Assignment

Family Token (*forthcoming*)

Fantasy Spirit Spouse

FAT Demons (The): *Breaking Demonic Curses*

The Fold (5 book series)

- The Fold (Book 1)
- Name Your Seed (Book 2)
- The Poor Attitudes of Money (3)
- Do Not Orphan Your Seed (4)
- For the Sake of the Gospel (5)

Fruit of the Womb:

Gates of Thanksgiving

Gathered

got HEALING? Verses for Life

got LOVE? Verses for Life

got HOPE? Verses for Life

got money?

How to Dental Assist

How to Dental Assit2: Be Productive, Not Wasteful

I Take It Back

Legacy

Let Me Have A Dollar's Worth

Level the Playing Field

Living for the NOW of God

Lose My Location
https://a.co/d/crD6mV9

Man Safari, *The*

Marriage Ed. Rules of Engagement & Marriage

Made Perfect in Love

Money Hunters: Beware of Those

Motherboard (The) - soul prosperity series

Name Your Seed

Occupy: *Until I Return*

Plantation Souls

Players Gonna Play

Power Money: Nine Times the Tithe

The Power of Wealth *(forthcoming)*

Powers Above

Marriage Ed.: Rules of Engagement & Marriage

Mulberry Tree, *The* https://a.co/d/6JP7KqK

Seasons of Grief

Seasons of Waiting

Seasons of War

Second Marriage, Third--, Any Marriage

Sift You Like Wheat

Spirits of Death, Hell & the Grave, Pass Over Me and My House

Soul Prosperity soul prosperity series 3

https://a.co/d/5p8YvCN

Souls Captivity soul prosperity series 2

The Spirit of Poverty

StarStruck

SUNBLOCK

The Swallowers: Thieves of Darkness (Book 3) https://a.co/d/4DxSZz6

Take It Back https://a.co/d/dZnVE25

This Is NOT That: How to Keep Demons from Coming at You

Throne of Grace: Courtroom Prayer

Time Is of the Essence

Too Many Wives: *Why You Have Lady Problems*

Tormenting Spirits https://a.co/d/dAogEJf

Toxic Souls

Triangular Power *(series)*

- Powers Above
- SUNBLOCK
- Do Not Swear by the Moon
- STARSTRUCK

Uncontested Doom

Unguarded House, *The*

Unseen Life, *The* (forthcoming)

Upgrade: How to Get Out of Survival Mode

- Toxic Souls (Book 2 of series)
- Legacy (Book 3 of series)

Warfare Prayer Against Beauty Curses

Warfare Prayer Against Poverty

The Wasters: *Thieves of Darkness (Book 2)* https://a.co/d/bs2UP7Y

What Have You to Declare? What Do You Have with You from Where You've Been?

When I Was a Child, I Prayed As a Child

When the Devourer is Rebuked

The Wilderness Romance
https://a.co/d/jfkMlnj

- The Social Wilderness
- The Sexual Wilderness
- The Spiritual Wilderness

The Wilderness Romance series is not a romance novel series. These books are about relationships with people who are still in the **Wilderness**, how to avoid them, or what to do if you've married one.

Series:

The Fold (a series on Godly finances)
https://a.co/d/4hz3unj

Soul Prosperity Series https://a.co/d/bz2M42q

Thieves of Darkness series

Triangular Powers https://a.co/d/aUCjAWC

Upgrade (series) *How to Get Out of Survival Mode*
https://a.co/d/aTERhX0